HEROES OF HISTORY

# WILLIAM PENN

## *Unit Study*
### Curriculum Guide

## JANET & GEOFF BENGE

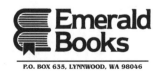

P.O. BOX 635, LYNNWOOD, WA 98046

Emerald Books are distributed through YWAM Publishing. For a full list of titles, including other great biographies and unit study curriculum guides, visit our website at www.ywampublishing.com or call 1-800-922-2143.

**William Penn: A Unit Study Curriculum Guide**
Copyright © 2004 by The Emerald Book Company

10  09  08  07  06  05  04      10 9 8 7 6 5 4 3 2 1

Published by Emerald Books
P.O. Box 635
Lynnwood, Washington 98046

ISBN 1-883002-87-7

**Printed in Germany.**

# Contents

# WILLIAM PENN

## 1644–1718

# William Penn:
# A Unit Study Curriculum Guide

This unit study guide is designed to accompany the book *William Penn: Liberty and Justice for All* from the Heroes of History series by Janet and Geoff Benge. It provides the schoolteacher and homeschooling parent with ways to use the book as a vehicle for teaching or reinforcing various curriculum areas, including

- Creative writing.
- Drama.
- Movie critiquing.
- Reading comprehension.
- Essay writing.
- History and geography concepts.

As there are more ideas than could possibly be used in one unit, it is the parent/teacher's job to sift through the ideas and select those that best fit the needs of the student or students.

The activities recommended in this unit study guide are

- Reflective of a wide range of learning styles.
- Designed for both group and individual study.
- Suitable for a range of grade levels and abilities.

## Learning Styles

Choose those activities that are best suited to your student or students. For example, when studying the physical features of a state, a kinesthetic learner may learn best by producing a three-dimensional clay model representing the physical features of the state, whereas a visual learner may find it more meaningful to produce a poster map of the state for the classroom wall.

## Group or Individual Study

While the activities contained in this unit study guide are designed to be carried out by a student working alone, instructions are also provided for adapting an activity for a group.

## Grade Levels/Abilities

As you thumb through this unit study guide, you will note that grade levels are not assigned to particular activities, though some areas—essay topics, for example—progress from the simple to the complex. This approach has been taken because students of varying grade levels can undertake most of the activities. For example, one of the activities asks students to imagine themselves as William Penn and write a series of journal entries on the journey to America that detail his plans for Pennsylvania. A fourth grader doing this activity might list details such as making treaties with Indians, planning Philadelphia, and finding land for a house. An older student would be able to add many details about why he was so eager to make treaties even though he already owned the land. The older student could then analyze William Penn's desire to transform the "Holy Experiment" into the perfect place to live. Using the same activities and instructions, each student will create work appropriate to his or her age and cognitive ability.

In the center of this unit study guide, you will find two foldout pages. These pages contain two maps, a timeline, and a fact sheet to be filled out by the student. The maps, timeline, and fact sheet are designed to be photocopied onto individual pages so that each student can store them in his or her folder. They are for use with the social studies section of this unit study guide (chapter 6).

Before you begin teaching from this unit study guide, please read through each section. You may wish to highlight the activities that appeal to you or that your students would enjoy or be challenged by. Many teachers find it useful to plan the culminating event (see chapter 8) first, then select a range of learning activities that lend themselves to this event.

For the sake of brevity in the instructions that accompany each section, the word *teacher* includes the homeschooling parent and the word *student* refers to a child either in a traditional classroom or in a homeschool environment.

—— *1* ——

# Key Quotes

The authors have selected ten quotes that can be used alongside or as part of this unit study. These could be used in the following ways:

*Memorization.* The teacher can assign one or all of the quotes to be memorized during the course of the study. A chart could track which students have memorized which quotes.

*Meaning.* The quotes can be used to spark conversation on various aspects of William Penn's life. This can then be translated into action by having students form groups and present one of the quotes to the class in a creative manner. Students could make up a skit to illustrate the meaning of the quote or present a one-act play showing how the quote was relevant in the life of William Penn.

*Display.* Students could design a plaque, wall hanging, or banner, with one of the quotes written on it. This could be hung in a prominent place while the unit study is under way and used for decoration during the culminating event.

"If you want to be free, there is but one way; it is to guarantee an equally full measure of liberty to all your neighbors. There is no other."

—*Carl Schurz*

"They that can give up essential liberty to obtain a little temporary safety deserve neither liberty nor safety."

—*Benjamin Franklin*

"No pain, no palm; no thorns, no throne; no gall, no glory; no cross, no crown."

—*William Penn*

"We must remember that a right lost to one is lost to all."

—*William Reece Smith Jr.*

"The two most powerful warriors are patience and time."

—*Chinese proverb*

"Strength does not come from winning. Your struggles develop your strengths. When you go through hardships and decide not to surrender, that is strength."

—*Arnold Schwarzenegger*

"The only people who achieve much are those who want knowledge so badly that they seek it while the conditions are still unfavorable. Favorable conditions never come."

—*C. S. Lewis*

⟨∞⟩

"So whatever you wish that others would do to you, do also to them."

—*Jesus Christ* (ESV)

⟨∞⟩

"Guard with jealous attention the public liberty. Suspect everyone who approaches that jewel."

—*Thomas Paine*

⟨∞⟩

"Whenever you find yourself on the side of the majority, it is time to pause and reflect."

—*Mark Twain*

# — 2 —

# Display Corner

Many students will enjoy collecting and displaying objects related to the times and places in which William Penn lived. It is motivational to designate a corner of the room, including a table or desk and wall space, that can be used for this purpose. Keep some index cards on the table and encourage students to label their contributions, including as much information as possible about where each object came from, what it is used for, and who would use it.

Encourage students to ask their parents and friends if they have anything relevant (but not valuable) from Pennsylvania or England that they could bring to class. A visit to the local library to find books on Pennsylvania might yield some interesting display items. Following is a list of items students (or you) might like to display. Of course, there are many more options.

- Large maps of areas where William Penn lived
- A copy of part or all of the charter of Pennsylvania (see www.yale.edu/lawweb/avalon/states/pa01.htm)
- Articles or books about William Penn, Lord Baltimore, King Charles I, King Charles II, Oliver Cromwell, King James II, King William and Queen Mary, Queen Anne, Samuel Pepys, John Bunyan (author of *Pilgrim's Progress),* and George Fox (founder of the Quakers)
- Books on Native American tribes of the Northeast
- Information about the American colonies in the 1600s
- Information about the state of Pennsylvania
- A map of the city of Philadelphia (original and/or current)
- Facsimiles of old stamps, coins, or money from William Penn's era
- A picture of Pennsylvania's coat of arms (see www.50states.com/flag/paflag.htm)
- Information on the plague and fire of London
- A picture of the Tower of London and information about its history
- A timeline showing the English monarchs who reigned during William Penn's life and their religious affiliation
- A family tree for William Penn
- Illustrations of ships from the 1600s
- A copy of the Bill of Rights

# —— 3 ——

# Chapter Questions

There are four questions related to each chapter of *William Penn: Liberty and Justice for All*:
1. A vocabulary question drawn from the text and referenced to a page in the book
2. A factual question arising from the text
3. A question to gauge the level of a student's comprehension
4. An open-ended question seeking an opinion or interpretation

These questions are designed for students to complete on their own. They are best answered after a student finishes reading each chapter in the book. Answers to the first three questions for each chapter are given in Appendix B of this guide. The answer to the fourth question is open-ended and needs to be evaluated separately. Since question four deals with a student's interpretation or opinions, it is a good question on which to base a group discussion. Keep in mind that there are no right or wrong answers to question four, only positions that a student should be able to justify.

To gain maximum benefit from the questions, the students should write full-sentence answers and not just one or two words. For example, in response to the question "Who succeeded Oliver Cromwell in power after his death?" students should write, "Oliver Cromwell was succeeded by his son Richard," and not just "his son."

Each vocabulary question asks the students to use the new word in a sentence. Make sure their sentences clearly demonstrate the meaning of the vocabulary word.

As a supplement to answering the questions, students may write a short summary of each chapter or write a response to the chapter in their journal. This could involve the students writing about how they relate to William Penn's actions, noting how they think they would react in a similar situation, and speculating as to what might happen next in the story.

## Chapter One

1. What does *recant* mean (page 13)? Use this word in a sentence.
2. Where was William locked up?
3. What did William mean when he said, "My prison shall be my grave before I will budge a jot"(page 13)?
4. What are two aspects of William's character that are evident in this chapter? Give examples of both.

## Chapter Two

1. What does *curtailed* mean (page 17)? Use this word in a sentence.

2. How did political leadership change in Britain when King Charles was executed?
3. How did Cromwell's beliefs about religious freedom change after he stepped into leadership?
4. Do you think a government benefits its people by supporting certain religions and repressing others? Explain your answer.

## Chapter Three

1. What does *transfixed* mean (page 34)? Use this word in a sentence.
2. Who succeeded Oliver Cromwell in power after his death?
3. How did Quaker beliefs about communicating with God differ from those of the Church of England?
4. Admiral Penn claimed that the English peasants were better workers than the Irish peasants. Do you think this was true, or was there some other reason he wanted English peasants in Macroom? Explain your answer.

## Chapter Four

1. What does *beleaguered* mean (page 40)? Use this word in a sentence.
2. What appointment did Prince Charles give to Admiral Penn?
3. What about Admiral Penn's political connections would cause the Puritans at Oxford to look at William with suspicion?
4. When William was watching Prince Charles's procession, Samuel Pepys said, "You have a bright future before you, boy. Be sure you make the most of it"

(page 46). Put yourself in William's place. What "bright future" would you pursue? Explain your choice.

## Chapter Five

1. What is a vagabond (page 53)? Use this word in a sentence.
2. What was Lincoln's Inn?
3. Why did William hate to tell his father that he was at the Protestant school?
4. Admiral Penn thought he was helping William when he tried to steer him away from Quaker beliefs. Why might he have thought this?

## Chapter Six

1. What does *countenance* mean (page 67)? Use this word in a sentence.
2. What tragedy struck England in September of 1666?
3. Why did the Quaker woman at the store doubt that William would need anything there?
4. Some historians consider it out of character for William to sign up for a battle. What do you think might have motivated him to do so?

## Chapter Seven

1. What does *persecution* mean (page 78)? Use this word in a sentence.
2. Who offered to go with William to meet with his father?
3. Why was it significant that William took off his sword and gave it away?
4. Why do you think Admiral Penn so strongly opposed William's decision to become a Quaker?

## Chapter Eight

1. What does *barrage* mean (page 86)? Use this word in a sentence.
2. What convinced King Charles II to release William?
3. What incident showed that there was no separation between church and state in England at that time?
4. Do you think William expected to end up in the Tower of London when he began his new life as a Quaker? Explain your answer.

## Chapter Nine

1. What is an indictment (page 96)? Use this word in a sentence.
2. What charge did the jury find William guilty of?
3. Why did the lord mayor order that hats be placed on the Quakers' heads in court?
4. The book is subtitled *Liberty and Justice for All.* How just do you think the English court system was at the time of William's trial? Explain your answer.

## Chapter Ten

1. What does *prevailed* mean (page 118)? Use this word in a sentence.
2. Who is the author of *Pilgrim's Progress*?
3. What did the lord chief justice mean by his statement "A judge may try to open the eyes of the jurors, but not lead them by the nose" (pages 109–110)?
4. Why do you think the Test Act was such a blow to William?

## Chapter Eleven

1. What is a proprietor (page 121)? Use this word in a sentence.

2.  How large was the plot of land that was granted to William estimated to be?
3.  What did William mean when he wrote to the Pennsylvania settlers, "I shall not usurp the right of any or oppress his person" (page 122)?
4.  If William and his father had not reconciled, do you think Pennsylvania would have been founded? Explain your answer.

## Chapter Twelve

1.  What does *confiscated* mean (page 137)? Use this word in a sentence.
2.  What name did William give to the new city, and what does the name mean?
3.  Why did William pay for property to build his home on when, according to the law, he already owned it?
4.  Do you think William found the Native Americans or his English neighbor Lord Baltimore easier to deal with? Why?

## Chapter Thirteen

1.  What is an edict (page 149)? Use this word in a sentence.
2.  Which couple became king and queen when King James II left for France?
3.  Why did William go into hiding in February 1689?
4.  What do you think it would be like to live in a country where the government was allowed to persecute you for your religious beliefs? What do you know about the countries where this still happens today?

## Chapter Fourteen

1.  What is a tenant (page 163)? Use this word in a sentence.

2. Who was told to take over the colony of Pennsylvania?

3. Why was the title *Some Fruits of Solitude* appropriate for William's essays?

4. The title of this chapter is "Losses and Gains." What do you think was the most significant thing William lost in this chapter and the most significant thing he gained? Explain your answer.

## Chapter Fifteen

1. What does *skeptical* mean (page 172)? Use this word in a sentence.

2. What did William discuss with the colonial governors at the conference?

3. What did William mean when he wrote, "I only wish myself…no Englishman" (page 174)?

4. When William left for England in 1701, he planned to return within six months. In light of his last visit, do you think this was realistic? Why or why not?

## Chapter Sixteen

1. What does *embodied* mean (page 188)? Use this word in a sentence.

2. How did King William die?

3. How did William collect taxes from Pennsylvania?

4. Who do you think caused William more trouble, the Fords or his son, "William the Waster"? Explain your answer.

## Chapter Seventeen

1. What does *lethargic* mean (page 195)? Use this word in a sentence.

2. Where did William retreat to after his stroke?

3. Why were all royal charters dissolved after the Revolutionary War?
4. Do you think that William, in the five years before he died, imagined that the American colonies would unite and adopt many of his ideas about liberty and justice? Explain your answer.

# ——— *4* ———

# Student Explorations

Student explorations are a variety of activities that are appropriate to a wide range of learning styles. These activities consist of the following:

*Essay Questions.* These are questions that can be used as ideas for writing essays. Students can either be assigned a topic or choose their own from the list. The simplest essay topics appear first, followed in order by those that are more complex.

*Creative Writing.* This includes writing such things as newspaper articles, poems, letters, résumés, journals, and songs.

*Hands-on Projects.* These are various kinds of projects, such as charts and graphs, models, comic strips, family crests, mottoes, dioramas, book covers, and mobiles.

*Audio/Visual Projects.* These involve such things as using a tape recorder to conduct a mock interview or to produce a radio play or commercial, or using still and video cameras to create dramatic presentations.

*Arts and Crafts.* These include a variety of art and craft forms.

*[Note on group projects: All the suggestions described below are individual learning activities. However, some of the activities have bracketed paragraphs such as this one that offer suggestions on how the activity can be adapted for class or group use.]*

## Essay Questions

1.  Use the book to study the relationship between William Penn and his father, Sir Admiral William Penn, and write an essay explaining their disagreements and final reconciliation.

2.  Both William Penn and his father were prisoners in the Tower of London. Research the history of the tower, and write a report on another prisoner who interests you.

3.  Research the plague and fire of London, and write a report on them that includes their effects on the people of London.

4.  One character trait that William Penn possessed was humility. Discuss three instances in which William showed humility, and explain what resulted.

5.  Few people ever experience betrayal to the extent that William Penn endured it at the hands of Philip and Bridget Ford. How do you think William was able to go on without becoming hostile or seeking revenge? Write an essay using references from the text to support your answer.

6.  What conditions and laws did William Penn encounter as a child and young man that may have influenced the

type of colony he wanted to lead in the "New World"? How did his principles for governing Pennsylvania address those issues? Write an essay using references from the text to support your argument.

7. William Reece Smith Jr. said, "We must remember that a right lost to one is lost to all." Explain what this quote means and how it applies to William Penn and to us today.

8. The Bill of Rights was written seventy years after William Penn's death. Using a copy of the Bill of Rights as a reference, explain how the need for at least three of these rights can be illustrated by William Penn's negative experiences in England. (The Bill of Rights can be found at http://memory.loc.gov/const/bor.html.)

9. Thomas Jefferson, influential in the formation of the United States, called William Penn "the greatest lawgiver the world has produced." Research and write an essay showing the influence of Penn's Charter of Privileges and ideas of liberty, justice, fairness, and tolerance on the U.S. Constitution and Bill of Rights. (The Charter of Privileges can be found at www.yale.edu/lawweb/avalon/states/pa07.htm. The Constitution and Bill of Rights can be found at http://memory.loc.gov/const/const.html.)

## Creative Writing

1. Imagine you are William Penn's mother. Write a poem describing the hopes you have for him when he is born.

2. Imagine you are a reporter covering the case between

William Penn and Bridget Ford. Write a newspaper article about the trial, being sure to use quotations and to include both sides of the story.

*[If you allocate different events in William Penn's life to different students, your class can create an imaginary newspaper that covers the whole of his life.]*

3.  Draw a large profile of William Penn's head. Inside it write some of his important ideas and quotations.

4.  Write a résumé for William Penn that shows why he was a suitable candidate to be given the charter to Pennsylvania.

5.  Choose six places where William Penn lived (or found himself), and draw a postcard of each. Make your drawing as accurate as you can to the time period. Then, pretending you are William Penn, write a note on the back of each one, as if you were writing from that place. Be sure to include whom you are writing to.

6.  Imagining you are William Penn, write a series of journal entries during his journey to America that detail his plans for Pennsylvania.

*[If you allocate different events or chapters to different students, your class can create an imaginary journal that covers the whole of William Penn's life.]*

7.  Write a eulogy (a speech that praises someone after his or her death) that one of the Indian chiefs might have given for William Penn. Be sure to include the character traits and actions that the chief admired in William and give the eulogy an appropriate title.

## Hands-on Projects

1. Make a bound book (comb-bound, stapled, sewed, or punched), and draw one letter of the alphabet on each page. Find one word that describes something about William Penn that starts with each letter. Write the word on the appropriate page, explain why it is relevant to William Penn's life, and illustrate the word using drawings or pictures from magazines, newspapers, or computer printouts. (Examples: A = Agile. William liked to join in the Native Americans' games, and he often won races and wrestling contests. B = Benefactor. William was a benefactor to the Quakers in England.)

2. Make a mobile that displays five to seven objects that were important in William Penn's life. Attach to each a brief explanation of why it was important.

3. Using the book, make a family tree for William Penn, showing his parents, siblings, wives, and children. Be sure to record each person's birth and death dates if given. (The website at http://www.williampenn.org gives excellent information on his family, all the way through his great-grandchildren.)

4. Make a papier-mâché or clay topographical model of Pennsylvania. On it label the major rivers, mountain ranges, plains, ocean, and places William Penn lived or visited.

5. Make a poster that commemorates William Penn. Make sure it shows why Americans should remember him.

6.   Make a brochure that could have been used to encourage English people to immigrate to Pennsylvania. (Keep in mind the sort of people William Penn was trying to attract.)

## Audio/Visual Projects

1.   Using a video camera, make a production of *William Penn: This Is Your Life*. Select key people from Penn's life to participate, and be sure to have them remind him of memorable moments.

     *[This is most easily done as a group activity.]*

2.   Write a one-act play about an event in William Penn's life, such as the trial for causing a riot on Gracechurch Street or meeting with Indians to make a treaty. Act out the play, and videotape it to show later.

     *[This can be done as a group project by having several students portray characters, with one student acting as William.]*

3.   Imagine you are a tour guide in London in 1718 (the year William Penn died). Write a script describing some of the places you would show people interested in learning more about his life and explaining their importance. Read the script onto an audiotape. (Use sound effects and vivid descriptions, and make the recording as interesting as you can to keep your audience's attention.)

4.   Create a series of mock interviews with people who were significant in William Penn's life. Ask these people questions about him to find out what they think about him, his beliefs, and his plan for Pennsylvania. Record the interviews on audiotape or videotape.

     *[This can be an individual or a group effort.]*

## Arts and Crafts

1. Obtain an early map of Philadelphia. Make a model of William Penn's plan for the city. (A map is available at http://xroads.virginia.edu/~CAP/PENN/pnplan.html.)

2. Use a coil technique in clay modeling to make a replica of the Liberty Bell.

3. Learn some basic calligraphy techniques and use them to copy part or all of the charter of Pennsylvania. (See www.yale.edu/lawweb/avalon/states/pa01.htm.)

4. When William Penn was in college, students sewed together their own notebooks. Find some textured paper and cardboard to sew together to make your own notebook or journal.

5. Learn about Indian beadwork (wampum), and attempt to create some yourself. (For history and instructions see www.nativetech.org/wampum/wamphist.htm.)

# — 5 —

# Community Links

M any communities have rich resources of people and places to which students can be exposed to help them learn about and appreciate other time periods and the experiences of other people. It is well worth the effort to find out what your community has to offer in regard to the unit you are studying. For example, you may be able to visit a Quaker meetinghouse to learn more about Quaker beliefs or invite a lawyer to visit your class to discuss current laws affecting religious freedom. If you are unable to take a field trip to visit some of these people and places, it is often possible to have visitors come to the classroom. Whether you take a field trip or invite someone to your classroom, such activities need to be flanked by sound educational choices; otherwise, much of the event's educational value will not be realized. The following three steps will help students derive the greatest educational value from a field trip or classroom visit.

## Step One: Preparation

Students should always research the topic before they begin a field trip or classroom interview. In doing so, they will be ready to ask intelligent questions based upon a sound knowledge of their topic. For example, if you are going to invite a Quaker to talk to the class, students should learn ahead of time about some basic Quaker beliefs and have a general idea of the role Quakers played in American history.

As the teacher, you need to give the students a clear idea as to why they are going on a field trip and what they are expected to produce with their findings. For example, you might say to them, "We are going to visit a Quaker meetinghouse and a cathedral. I want you to note three differences and three similarities between them. When you get back to class, you will make a poster highlighting these comparisons."

Prior to the event, students should be encouraged to compile lists of questions to which they want answers, stemming from what they have already learned. They should carry a clipboard with them to write down answers, draw sketches, and note observations. (For less motivated students, a simple worksheet of activities to be completed on the field trip itself may be a good idea.) Such activities reinforce the idea that the field trip is a serious educational event and that the student is there to gather information, not just be a sightseer.

## Step Two: The Event

During the field trip or classroom visit, make sure that the students remain on task. Insist that they be respectful of property and other people at all times. Make sure that you have a spokesperson designated to thank whomever you talk to as well as the parents who help with the event.

## Step Three: Processing and Reflection

Students should be given time to process the information they have gathered from their field trip or classroom visit and reflect on it, both individually and as a class. This can take many forms: making flowcharts or diagrams of what they have learned, editing interviews for articles or audiovisual presentations, writing reports, and making booklets. Something as simple as a class book called *Did You Know?*, in which each student writes down one fact he or she learned from the field trip, can serve as an effective reflection tool.

## Suggested Community Links

People in the community are some of the best resources of all. Consider asking one of the following people to be a guest speaker in your classroom.

*Resident of Philadelphia.* Perhaps there is someone in your community who has lived in Philadelphia or elsewhere in Pennsylvania and knows some of the history of the area. Ask the person to bring pictures to add interest to his or her talk.

*Quaker.* Check your phone book for Quaker meetings in your area, and contact someone about visiting your class to explain Quaker beliefs and how they have impacted American history and law.

*Attorney.* A lawyer could explain the laws we have in the United States that protect individual religious freedom and why the laws are still so important.

*Human Rights Activist, Immigrant, Missionary, et al.* Invite someone to speak with your class who is knowledgeable about current religious persecution in one or more nations. Depending on the person's knowledge, he or she could describe the global situation or the experiences of people in one particular nation and explain what students can do to help people suffering persecution today.

You might also consider taking your class to visit one of the following locations.

*Museum.* Perhaps there is a museum in your community that you could visit to learn about the colonial time period. (If you live in one of the original colonial states, you might be able to find local reenactments of colonial life.)

*Courthouse.* Many courthouses offer tours and allow students to ask questions about the law.

*Quaker Meetinghouse.* To help students understand the simple practice of faith that William Penn believed in, you could tour a traditional Quaker meetinghouse (which is very simple) and contrast it to a cathedral (which you could also visit).

# — 6 —

# Social Studies

The social studies section is divided into five categories, each with suggestions on how to use the material given. The categories are briefly described below.

*Places.* This section covers significant places related to the story and named in the text of the book *William Penn: Liberty and Justice for All.*

*Terms/Vocabulary.* This section gives ideas for studying some of the terms used in the book.

*Geographical Characteristics.* This section contains suggestions for mapping some of the physical characteristics of Pennsylvania.

*Timeline.* This section allows students to research the time period in which William Penn lived by plotting historical events.

*Conceptual Questions.* This section provides the teacher with conceptual social studies questions related to the book.

# William Penn
# Fact Sheet

**Full Name:** _____

**Nickname:** _____

**Birth Date:** _____

**Birthplace:** _____

**Parents:** _____

**Siblings:** _____

**Spouse:** _____

**Children:** _____

**Profession:** _____

**Important Achievements:** _____

_____

_____

_____

**Date of Death:** _____

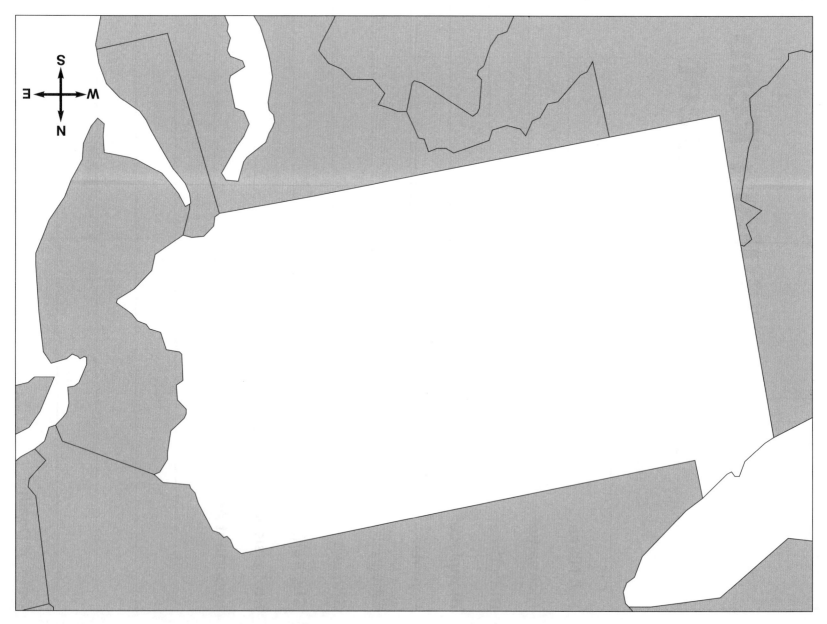

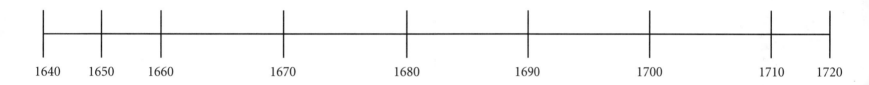

| 1640 | 1650 | 1660 | 1670 | 1680 | 1690 | 1700 | 1710 | 1720 |

# Timeline

**Plot these important events from history and William Penn's life on the timeline above.**

Admiral Penn dies
Anne Stuart becomes queen of England
Battle of Boyne
Fire of London
Guli Penn dies
James II becomes king of England
King Charles killed
King Charles II dies

King Charles II signs charter for
   Pennsylvania
King William dies
King William's War begins
Oliver Cromwell dies
Penn family moves to Ireland
Plague of London
War of Spanish Succession

William and Mary become king and queen of England
William Penn's birth and death
William Penn's enrollment and expulsion from Oxford
William Penn's first arrival in Pennsylvania
William Penn goes to France
William Penn's imprisonment in Tower of London
William Penn's marriage to Guli Springett
William Penn's marriage to Hannah Callowhill

# United Kingdom and Ireland

Europe

N
W —|— E
S

## Places

The page number where the place is first mentioned is in parentheses. Students can undertake a range of activities with these place names. They can

- Locate and mark the places on the relevant map. (Maps for this purpose are located in the foldout section of this guide.)
- Note other points, such as their absolute location (latitude and longitude), then observe how this location compares to other locations mentioned in the book. For example, calculate which location is closer to the equator or the North Pole.
- Calculate the relative locations of various places mentioned in the book. For example, how far is it from Pennsbury, Pennsylvania, to New Castle, Delaware, or from London, England, to Philadelphia, Pennsylvania?
- Construct a key to show current population densities in England, Delaware, and Pennsylvania.
- Explore how some of the place names have changed since the time of the story, and give reasons for such changes.
- Pinpoint the places on a large wall map in the classroom. Students can then use index cards to write why the various places are mentioned in the story. Each card could be pinned to the wall, with a length of yarn connecting it to the appropriate place on the map.

## Places in England

London (12)                 Bristol (191)
Wanstead (17)               Berkshire (194)
Worminghurst (170)

## Places in America

New Castle, Delaware (130)   Philadelphia, Pennsylvania (136)
Upland (Chester),            Pennsbury, Pennsylvania (136)
   Pennsylvania (134)

## Other places

The Netherlands (19)        Macroom, Ireland (30)
Scotland (19)               Paris, France (55)
Hispaniola (23)             Cork, Ireland (64)

## Terms/Vocabulary

Following is a list of terms used in the book. The page number where the term is first used is in parentheses. The list covers terms ranging from the simple to the advanced. Students can use this list to

- Define and memorize the terms. You may find it helpful to asterisk or highlight in some way those terms you think are appropriate for your students. If they know the meaning of all but five of the terms, have them learn only those five. Conversely, if they are unfamiliar with most of the terms, choose a realistic number for each student to explore and learn.
- Produce an individual or class reference book of terms. Assign each student a number of terms to write a definition for or, where possible, depict in a sketch. From this research, a book of definitions can be made, allotting one page for each definition. This

book could be added to throughout the year. (Students may need a dictionary to help them with this activity.)

- Play reinforcement games. For example, write some terms from the list below on index cards and have students take turns pairing them with definitions written on other index cards.

*Terms/vocabulary*

Roundheads (16)
parliament (16)
commonwealth (16)
Catholics (18)
Protestant (18)
Puritan (18)
peasants (31)
brigade (31)
lowlands (31)
Quakers (32)
royalists (43)
black plague (61)
dissenters (114)
treason (114)
boundary (119)
colony (121)
traders (123)
quitrent (124)
settlers (127)
trading post (134)

Lenni Lenape (134)
village (135)
wampum (136)
parcels (138)
inhabited (139)
latitude (140)
cultivated (141)
population (143)
industries (143)
merchant (147)
Huguenot (149)
Anabaptist (149)
monarchs (153)
tenement (160)
militia (163)
confluence (169)
territories (173)
proprietorship (173)
Crown colony (173)

## Geographical Characteristics

Have students use an atlas to locate the following and then mark them on the blank map of Pennsylvania from the foldout section in the center of the book:

- The following eleven rivers in Pennsylvania, their sources, and their courses: Delaware, Juniata, Lehigh, Schuylkill, Susquehanna, Ohio, Allegheny, Beaver, Monongahela, Conemaugh, and Youghiogheny
- The seven major geographical regions: Erie Lowland, Allegheny Plateau, Appalachian Ridge and Valley Region, Blue Ridge, Piedmont, New England Upland, and the Atlantic Coastal Plain
- Mount Davis, the highest point in Pennsylvania at 3,213 feet
- The eight largest cities in Pennsylvania: Philadelphia, Pittsburgh, Erie, Allentown, Scranton, Upper Darby, Reading, and Bethlehem
- Lake Erie
- The latitude and longitude lines that bisect Pennsylvania
- The states with which Pennsylvania shares borders: Maryland, West Virginia, New York, Ohio, Delaware, and New Jersey

## Timeline

Have students plot important events from history and from William's life on the timeline provided on the foldout page in the center of this study guide. Students can work in groups to create a larger timeline for the classroom wall.

## Conceptual Questions

The following questions are ordered from the simple to the complex. Using these questions, you could ask students to

- Write one or more paragraphs to answer each question.

- Present an oral report to the class on one of the questions.
- Discuss the answer(s) to a question or questions in a group context.

*Questions to ponder*

1. Name and locate two states that are larger than Pennsylvania, two that are about the same size, and two that are smaller.

2. Study a physical map of Pennsylvania. Where do you think most of the population would live? Why? Use a population map to test your hypothesis. Were you right or wrong? Explain.

3. Early in its history Pennsylvania was known for the friendly relations between Native Americans and settlers that William Penn was careful to establish. Where do the Lanape people live today, and what conditions made them move?

4. Pennsylvania is known as the Keystone State. Explain why and how the state has lived up to that name throughout its history.

5. What traces of early Quaker influences can still be found in Pennsylvania today?

6. Religious persecution like William Penn suffered in England still occurs in many nations today. Research a nation whose citizens currently experience persecution for their religious beliefs. Does the nation have any laws similar to those in effect in England during Penn's lifetime? What appears to motivate the persecution? How are the persecuted responding?

# ──── 7 ────

# Related Themes to Explore

Any unit study has natural links to many other topics that can also be explored. While it is impossible to pursue all such links in this context, the spoke diagram on the next page shows some related topics that students might find interesting to study in conjunction with William Penn.

There are two ways you might integrate some of these links into your classroom. Some teachers and parents have the flexibility to choose the topics their students study and even alter their selections partway through the year. If you are able to do this, use the theme wheel to help identify other topics you might like to explore following this unit. For example, after studying William Penn, your class might become interested in other famous characters of the American colonies or the English monarchy.

Other teachers and parents are locked into a less flexible curriculum. If this is your situation, you may still have the ability to change the order in which various topics are taught. Look through the list of topics to see whether any coincide with topics you have already scheduled for later in the year. If so, consider teaching these topics closer to this unit so that cross-curriculum learning can take place.

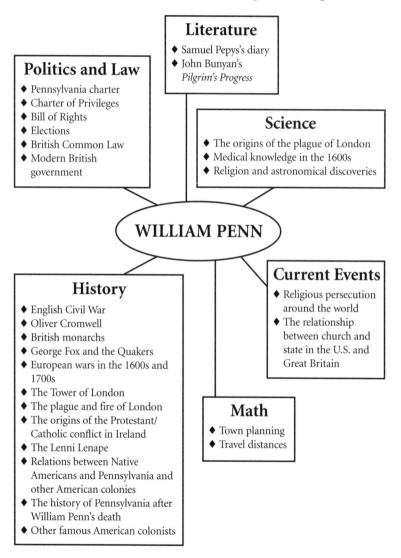

**Literature**
- ◆ Samuel Pepys's diary
- ◆ John Bunyan's *Pilgrim's Progress*

**Politics and Law**
- ◆ Pennsylvania charter
- ◆ Charter of Privileges
- ◆ Bill of Rights
- ◆ Elections
- ◆ British Common Law
- ◆ Modern British government

**Science**
- ◆ The origins of the plague of London
- ◆ Medical knowledge in the 1600s
- ◆ Religion and astronomical discoveries

**WILLIAM PENN**

**History**
- ◆ English Civil War
- ◆ Oliver Cromwell
- ◆ British monarchs
- ◆ George Fox and the Quakers
- ◆ European wars in the 1600s and 1700s
- ◆ The Tower of London
- ◆ The plague and fire of London
- ◆ The origins of the Protestant/ Catholic conflict in Ireland
- ◆ The Lenni Lenape
- ◆ Relations between Native Americans and Pennsylvania and other American colonies
- ◆ The history of Pennsylvania after William Penn's death
- ◆ Other famous American colonists

**Current Events**
- ◆ Religious persecution around the world
- ◆ The relationship between church and state in the U.S. and Great Britain

**Math**
- ◆ Town planning
- ◆ Travel distances

# 8

# Culminating Event

As adults, we like having a reason to learn something. We learn a new computer program so that we can balance our checking account, a song so that we can sing it at a wedding, or the rudiments of another language so that we are able to find our way around in a foreign country. Students have the same need for purpose in their learning. It is valid but not very motivating to tell a student that he or she needs to gather and learn information to pass a test or move up a grade. It is much more motivating for a student when he or she has some other, more meaningful, goal in mind. This goal can be a specific forum through which each student can express his or her newly acquired knowledge. We believe that part of a teacher's role is to provide such a forum, which we call "the culminating event."

As the name implies, the culminating event marks the end of the unit study and gives a sense of closure to the topic. It also serves to put the students' new knowledge into a larger context that can be shared with others.

The culminating event can be as simple as inviting the class next door (or the homeschooled children down the street) to come hear poems and stories and view your students' written work. Conversely, the event could be as involved as hosting a parent/neighborhood dinner featuring songs, games, plays, and presentations on the life and achievements of William Penn.

No matter how simple or elaborate the culminating event is, make sure you have the broad outline of it in mind before planning the other activities for your unit study, since the two are integrally linked.

## Idea Sparks

Host a peace treaty celebration. William Penn signed treaties with the local Lenni Lenape Indians. One of the most important of these was at Shackamaxon. (See page 139 in the book.) Recreate the meeting, holding it outside under a spreading tree if possible. Divide the participants into Lenape Indians and William Penn's entourage. (One person needs to be William Penn and one Chief Tammamend, the chief who is referenced on page 139 in the book.) After an "official" ceremony and the handing over of wampum (see arts and crafts section), gold guilders, and blankets, enjoy a feast together.

The website www.delawaretribeofindians.nsn.us/ tells what the Lenni Lenape ate, how they dressed, and the stories they told. The site also has for sale a cassette and a CD of the Lenni Lenape language, Lenape songs, a cookbook, the Lenape seal, and a variety of objects with that seal on them. Around twenty simple phrases in the local Lenni Lenape language are also available on the site.

*Invitations.* These could have on them the coat of arms for Pennsylvania, a suitable wampum design, or the Lenape seal (see the aforementioned website).

*Food.* The traditional food of the Lenni Lenape includes salmon, herring, shellfish, turkey, duck, eggs, berries, corn, beans, squash, walnuts, hickory nuts, chestnuts, acorns, plums, persimmons, and butternuts. You could serve blackberry tea or a cold berry juice with the meal.

*Music.* Play Lenni Lenape music (ordered from the same website) during the meal. (You may be able to find some CDs of traditional northeastern Native American music at your local library.)

*Clothing.* Use children's picture books on William Penn or the website to show you the kinds of clothes the Lenni Lenape and the white settlers wore. A description of William Penn's dress is found on page 139 of the book.

*Oral Presentations.* Students can present poems, essays, reports, speeches, reviews, and journals that they have written during the course of the unit study.

*Displays.* Display other work, including artwork, map work, models, newspapers, and video interviews.

# Appendix A

# Books and Resources

This appendix is divided into six sections: (1) other biographies of William Penn, (2) related books, (3) related books in the Heroes of History series, (4) related movies and documentaries, (5) related articles from *National Geographic,* and (6) related Internet sites.

Many books about William Penn are written at a higher reading level than are the books in the Heroes of History series and therefore would be useful for a teacher to read for his or her own information as background for the unit. Students learn best by example, so consider reading one adult book to enrich your own understanding of the topic. Resources for younger children are also included, making it easy for younger family members or less capable readers to participate in the unit study at their own reading level.

Some of the books listed here are more difficult to obtain than others. If they are not available at your local bookstore, many of the titles can be located in secondhand bookstores or on the Internet. Most of the titles are also available through the national interlibrary loan service.

## Other Biographies of William Penn

All the biographies listed on the bibliography page of *William Penn: Liberty and Justice for All* are listed here, as well as others that may be of interest. Each listing has basic information on how to locate the book, including its ISBN or ASIN. The approximate intended age level of the reader is also given, along with the number of pages in each book and some comments to help you decide whether or not to include the book in your unit study.

| | |
|---|---|
| TITLE: | *William Penn: Apostle of Dissent* |
| Author: | Hans Fantel |
| Publisher: | William Morrow & Co., 1974 |
| ISBN: | 068821603X |
| Age Level: | Adult, 290 pages |

Synopsis: This book covers the life of Penn, although the later part of his life, particularly after he returns to England from America for the second time, is dealt with in a sketchy manner. The book contains an appendix with the author's commentary on how Penn and the Quakers fit into the greater Reformation movement, as well as an extensive bibliography. It also contains six photographs.

Comments: This book is useful in understanding not only Penn's life but also how his ideas fit into the development of ideas of liberty and justice. Because of this the author often digresses into explanations of historical events that can last several pages. Readers who have scant understanding of European history during the 1600s will find this book helpful in bringing context to Penn's story. The book is written in a straightforward, easy-to-understand manner.

TITLE:      *William Penn: Politics and Conscience*
Author:     Mary Maples Dunn
Publisher:   Princeton University Press, 1967
ASIN:      0691045747
Age Level:   Adult, 200 pages

Synopsis: This biography deals specifically with the theme of liberty of conscience and the role it played in the evolving relationship between government and monarchy during the 1600–1700s.

Comments: This book has a good index, extensive footnoting, and an academic feel. It would be useful for high school students who are studying American government or history.

TITLE:      *Remember William Penn 1644–1944*
Author:     Editorial Committee, William Penn Tercentenary Committee
Publisher:   Pennsylvania Historical Commission, 1944
ISBN:      None given
Age Level:   Adult, 173 pages

Synopsis: This is an eclectic book containing a biography of Penn, a chronology of his life, transcripts of some of the trials he was involved in, his *Fruits of Solitude* publication (a collection of his reflections and maxims), and an extensive bibliography. The book also has fifty-three illustrations that include photos of Pennsbury (reconstructed), original maps of Philadelphia, portraits of Penn and Guli, and copies of letters Penn wrote.

Comments: This book was commissioned by the governor of Pennsylvania to commemorate the three hundredth anniversary of the birth of Penn. It was compiled by an editorial committee of professionals interested in presenting a picture of Penn as a man and as the founder of an American state. It is well researched and well presented and would be a good resource.

TITLE:      *William Penn: A Biography*
Author:     Catherine Owens Peare

Publisher:     University of Michigan Press, 1966
ISBN:     0472061208
Age Level:     Adult, 448 pages

Synopsis: This is a very thorough biography of Penn. It deals with both the religious and political aspects of his life, and it contains extensive footnoting, an eleven-page general bibliography, a seven-page bibliography of Penn's writings, and a good index.

Comments: If you want one book that gives detail and breadth to Penn's story, this is the book to get. Peare has left no stone unturned to find the truth about Penn and expose any myths. She often gives the reasoning and research behind a particular conclusion, which can be very helpful. The only photo is a portrait of the young William Penn wearing armor.

TITLE:     *William Penn: Founder of Pennsylvania*
Author:     Ronald Syme
Illustrator:     William Stobbs
Publisher:     William Morrow and Co., 1966
ASIN:     9997507975
Age Level:     8–10 years, 95 pages

Synopsis: This book deals with Penn's life and takes a brief look at the colony of Pennsylvania after his death.

Comments: This is an interesting story for children. It has many black-and-white illustrations, including an early map of Philadelphia. It is written in a clear and concise manner, though oversimplification creates misleading implications.

TITLE:     *William Penn: Founder of Pennsylvania*
Author:     Steven Kroll
Illustrator:     Ronald Himler
Publisher:     Holiday House, 2000
ISBN:     823414396
Age Level:     7 years and up, 32 pages

Synopsis: This is a short biography of Penn illustrated with water-color paintings.

Comments: This beautifully written book is a great choice for younger children.

TITLE:          *William Penn: Quaker Hero*
Author:         Hildegarde Dolson
Illustrator:     Leonard Everett Fisher
Publisher:      Random House, 1961
ASIN:          800005XY2W
Age Level:      9 years and up, 186 pages

Synopsis: This biography of William Penn contains occasional pen-and-ink drawings.

Comments: This is an excellent book that is geared toward a younger audience than *William Penn: Liberty and Justice for All.*

TITLE:                *The Story of William Penn*
Author/Illustrator:   Aliki
Publisher:           Aladdin Library, 1994
ASIN:               0671886460
Age Level:          4–8 years, 32 pages

Synopsis: This short biography of Penn contains lively pen-and-ink drawings (some black and white, some color).

Comments: This book by Aliki, the well-loved writer and illustrator, is simply and powerfully written.

## Related Books

Listed in this section are seven other books that fit around the life of Penn, including two written by Penn himself. The listings include the ISBN or ASIN, age level, and comments.

Of course, there are many other books that relate in some way to this topic. Inside the back cover of this unit study guide, you may want to record the titles of other books you find particularly helpful.

TITLE:          *No Cross, No Crown*
Author:         William Penn
Publisher:      Destiny Image Publications, 2001
ISBN:           0970791917
Age Level:      Adult, 208 pages

Synopsis: This is Penn's most famous book, written in the Tower of London. Penn makes the case that faith in Jesus Christ is a personal quest and tells the stories of other dissenters.

Comments: This is great material, but younger readers will need help deciphering parts of it.

TITLE:          *Some Fruits of Solitude*
Author:         William Penn
Publisher:      Applewood Books, 1996
ISBN:           1557094330
Age Level:      Adult, 96 pages

Synopsis: This is another of Penn's famous books written while he was imprisoned in the Tower of London. In it he talks about his beliefs on religion and government.

Comments: As with the previous entry, the subject matter and vocabulary in this book may be difficult reading for younger students.

TITLE:          *The People Called Quakers: The Enduring Influence*
                *of a Way of Life and a Way of Thought*
Author:         D. Elton Trueblood
Publisher:      Friends United Press, 1997
ISBN:           0913408026
Age Level:      Adult, 298 pages

Synopsis: This book gives a good general commentary of the Quaker movement and its foundation, beliefs, and practices on both sides of the Atlantic.

Comments: This book is a little dry to inspire the average reader to read it from cover to cover, but it is well indexed and gives good insight into Quakers. It deals extensively with George Fox, William Penn, and his stepfather-in-law, Isaac Penington. If you want general answers to questions like "What is the inner light the Quakers talk of?" or "Why don't Quakers take up arms?" you will find them here.

| | |
|---|---|
| TITLE: | *The Quakers* (American Religious Experience) |
| Author: | Jean Kinney Williams |
| Publisher: | Franklin Watts, 1998 |
| ISBN: | 0531113779 |
| Age Level: | 10 years and up, 112 pages |

Synopsis: This is an informative book on the history and current practices of American Quakers.

Comments: This book is part of a series of books on American religious groups.

| | |
|---|---|
| TITLE: | *Friend: The Story of George Fox and the Quakers* |
| Author: | Jane Yolen |
| Publisher: | Houghton Mifflin, 1972 |
| ISBN: | 0816430187 |
| Age Level: | 9 years and up, 179 pages |

Synopsis: This is a biography about George Fox and the Quaker movement.

Comments: This biography is interesting and includes a map and illustrated frontispiece.

| | |
|---|---|
| TITLE: | *The World of William Penn* |
| Author: | Genevieve Foster |
| Publisher: | Macmillan Publishing, 1977 |
| ASIN: | 068415725X |
| Age Level: | 9 years and up, 192 pages |

Synopsis: This book is about various world events in the 1600s and 1700s. The first third of the book focuses on Penn.

Comments: This book takes a unique "horizontal history" approach to Penn's time period. The second half gives a wide-ranging look at what was happening in other places, such as Holland and China.

TITLE:          *Samuel Pepys: A Life*
Author:         Stephen Coote
Publisher:      Hodder & Stoughton, 2001
ISBN:           034075124X
Age Level:      Adult, 397 pages

Synopsis: This book tells the life story of Samuel Pepys, the renowned diarist from the 1600s. Stephen Coote weaves a narrative around the diaries and other sources to give complete coverage of Pepys's life. Diary entries include those about British events Penn lived through, including the plague and fire of London, and the ever-changing political scene. Coote also comments on "Young Penn" from time to time.

Comments: Two of the most remembered people in English history during the Cromwellian and Restoration periods were next-door neighbors. These two characters are William Penn and Samuel Pepys. In fact, Pepys was a secretary in the British navy under the command of Sir William Penn, William's father. This book is wonderfully written, and it gives an unparalleled window into the time period. But Samuel Pepys was no saint, and the book has some rather lurid scenes in it. It is a great book to read excerpts from or for older students to read. It also contains sixteen pages of photos, mainly portraits of Pepys and important men of his time.

## Related Heroes of History Books

TITLE:          *George Washington: True Patriot*
Authors:        Janet and Geoff Benge
Publisher:      Emerald Books, 2001
ISBN:           1883002818
Age Level:      10 years and up, 224 pages

Comments: William Penn's ideals and governance of Pennsylvania greatly influenced the founders of the United States, laying a foundation for freedom. As commander in chief of the Continental army, chairman of the Constitutional Convention, and first president, George Washington served the struggling United States when its birth, survival, and form hung in the balance.

TITLE:          *John Adams: Independence Forever*
Authors:        Janet and Geoff Benge
Publisher:      Emerald Books, 2002
ISBN:           1883002516
Age Level:      10 years and up, 213 pages

Comments: John Adams featured largely in the American Revolution and founding of the United States. He served overseas as an ambassador to the French and followed George Washington to become the second president of the United States. Adams outlived Washington by twenty-six years, providing the next slice of U.S. history.

## Related Movies and Documentaries

Listed in this section are one movie and three documentaries that relate to American colonialism or have some relationship to William Penn's life. These films are not MPA rated, and as with all unfamiliar material, it is prudent to preview them before showing them to the class.

Movies and documentaries are particularly useful in showing the visual details of another place and time period. As students watch, encourage them to study the clothing, weather, crops, terrain, and other geographical factors shown in the movie or documentary.

TITLE:          *William Penn and Pennsylvania*
Publisher:      Schlessinger Media
Type:           Color Live Action
Length:         23 minutes

Year:          1999
Rating:        NR

Comments: This movie is part of the Colonial Life for Children series by Schlessinger Media. It is very informative, and its relatively fast pace makes it a good choice for younger children. Teacher guides are included or available online at www.libraryvideo.com.

TITLE:         *Growth of the English Colonies: 1620–1700*
Publisher:     Rainbow
Type:          Documentary
Length:        25 minutes
Year:          1999
Rating:        NR

Comments: This documentary tells about the history of English colonialism, focusing on New England, the Mid-Atlantic region, and Maryland. It is well done and can provide a broad background for the Penn era. The religious and ethnic backgrounds of settlers, as well as differences between colonies, are covered.

TITLE:         *Lenape* (Indians of North America Series)
Publisher:     Schlessinger Media
Type:          Documentary
Length:        30 minutes
Year:          1994
Rating:        NR

Comments: This documentary provides an insightful look at the history and current lives of the Lenape. It starts with Penn and the Quakers and shows how the Lenape were pushed west as European settlement encroached upon their lands. This documentary is suitable for grades four through eight.

TITLE:         *The English Civil War*
Publisher:     Britannica
Type:          Documentary

Length:        38 minutes
Year:          1986
Rating:        NR

Comments: This documentary is suitable for high school students. It discusses the details of the English Civil War, concentrating on the reasons for the war, tactics used in various types of battles, the areas of occupation, and the outcome. This is a slower-paced production, but it will give the viewer an idea of the confusion that defined this war and the reason Oliver Cromwell emerged as the Roundhead leader.

## Related *National Geographic* Articles

Many magazines have articles related to this topic. We have chosen to reference *National Geographic* because it can provide contemporaneous commentary on many events related to the Heroes of History series and because it is widely available in libraries and schools throughout the country.

These articles and their accompanying photographs represent just some of those available that bear on aspects of Penn's life. They can be used in a variety of ways to support and reinforce this unit study. For example, you could have students read the 1932 article "The Historic City of Brotherly Love: Philadelphia, Born of Penn and Strengthened by Franklin, a Metropolis of Industries," and compare it with the 1983 article "They'd Rather Be in Philadelphia." Since both articles deal with the city of Philadelphia, students could discuss the historical changes in Philadelphia over the fifty-year period.

### *Articles about Pennsylvania*

TITLE:         "The Historic City of Brotherly Love: Philadelphia, Born of Penn and Strengthened by Franklin, a Metropolis of Industries"
Issue Date:    December 1932, pages 643–697

Description: This article provides a historical look at the city of Philadelphia, paying particular attention to the layout of the city and the deviations that have been made from Penn's original vision. It also has a good photograph of the Penn statue at City Hall.

TITLE:    "Philadelphia Houses a Proud Past"
Issue Date:  August 1960, pages 151–191

Description: This is a great article about the historic importance of Philadelphia. It includes information on why Penn laid out the city the way he did, its Revolutionary and Civil War significance, and its brief period as the capital of the United States.

TITLE:    "Pennsylvania: Faire Land of William Penn"
Issue Date:  June 1978, pages 730–767

Description: This article provides a historical look at the state of Pennsylvania. It has a very good map of the state showing historical sites (including battlefields like Gettysburg), industries, and physical features.

TITLE:    "They'd Rather Be in Philadelphia"
Issue Date:  March 1983, pages 314–343

Description: This article gives a general overview of Philadelphia, plus a very good map of Penn's original layout for the city.

TITLE:    "Diamond Delaware, Colonial Still: Tradition Rules the Three Lower Counties over Which William Penn and Lord Baltimore Went to Law"
Issue Date:  September 1935, pages 367–398

Description: This article chronicles the two-hundred-year-old dispute that began with Penn and Lord Baltimore over the boundaries of Delaware. It is clearly written for a story with so many twists and turns.

*Articles about other places where William Penn lived*

TITLE:        "The Penn Country in Sussex: Home of
                   Pennsylvania's Founder Abounds in Quaker
                   History and Memories of Adventurous Smugglers"
Issue Date:   July 1935, pages 59–90

Description: This is an article about the Sussex area in southern England where Penn spent much of his time. It includes photographs of the inside of some of the meetinghouses he attended and many interesting facts and legends about the area.

TITLE:        "The Living Tower of London"
Issue Date:   October 1993, pages 36–57

Description: This is a great article about the history of the Tower of London and the people who live and work in it today. It contains stunning photography.

## Related Internet Sites

The following websites may have been updated since this guide was published, and as a result, they may contain information not reviewed here. Because of this, it is vital that you investigate them before allowing your students to view them.

http://www.quakerinfo.com/quakpenn.html

This is a Quaker website that offers links to the text of most of Penn's pamphlets and existing letters. Chapter 2 ("Advice to His Children") is particularly interesting. The site also has online bookstore links for books on Quakers and Penn.

http://www.williampenn.org/

This site has an interesting biography, the second half of which focuses on what became of Penn's family and his property after he died.

www.pennsburymanor.org/

This is the official website of Pennsbury Manor, the recreated home of Penn. The site explains the manor's history and contains a diagram of the house and grounds that students can click on to learn more. It also describes programs available at Pennsbury.

www.delawaretribeofindians.nsn.us/

This is the website of the Delaware Indians. It features information on the Lenni Lenape, including Penn's land purchase from them. It tells what they ate, how they dressed, and the stories they told. It also offers for sale a cassette and a CD of the Lenni Lenape language, Lenape songs, a cookbook, and a variety of objects with the Lenni Lenape seal on them. Twenty or so simple phrases in the Lenape language are also available on the site.

www.yale.edu/lawweb/avalon/states/pa01.htm

This Yale Law School site contains the text of the Charter for the Province of Pennsylvania with which King Charles II granted William Penn the territory of Pennsylvania and the power to form the new colony's government and rule over it.

www.yale.edu/lawweb/avalon/states/pa07.htm

This Yale Law School site contains the text of the Charter of Privileges granted by William Penn to the Inhabitants of Pennsylvania. This is the farsighted framework of laws Penn put in place in the colony.

http://memory.loc.gov/const/const.html

The text of the U.S. Constitution and Bill of Rights can be found on this Library of Congress website.

# ——— *Appendix B* ———

# Answers to Chapter Questions

### Chapter One

1. *Recant* means to take back something that has been written or said.
2. William was locked up in the Tower of London.
3. William meant that he would not recant what he had written, even if it meant dying in prison.

### Chapter Two

1. *Curtailed* means to have cut something short.
2. Instead of having a king, Britain had a parliament and a commonwealth, with Oliver Cromwell as its leader.
3. Cromwell originally seemed to want religious freedom and tolerance, but once in power he used force to try to convert Irish Catholics to the Church of England.

### Chapter Three

1. *Transfixed* means rendered motionless, as with terror, amazement, or awe.
2. Oliver Cromwell was succeeded by his son Richard.

3. Quakers believed that people could be directly in touch with God, whereas the Church of England held that a mediator was necessary between people and God.

## Chapter Four

1. *Beleaguered* means surrounded with troubles.
2. Prince Charles made Admiral Penn a knight.
3. Puritan ideals were contrary to Royalist ideals, and because Admiral Penn had been loyal to the royalty and accepted the king's appointment, the Puritans at Oxford viewed William as a royalist.

## Chapter Five

1. A vagabond is a tramp or a drifter.
2. Lincoln's Inn was a school of law in London.
3. William hated to tell his father that he was at the Protestant school because his father had sent him to France to mix with wealthy people and forget about religious matters.

## Chapter Six

1. *Countenance* means bearing or manner.
2. The Fire of London occurred in September of 1666.
3. The woman doubted that William would need anything because the store sold "plain things" and William's clothing indicated a wealthy, elegant lifestyle.

## Chapter Seven

1. *Persecution* means harassment or oppression for one's beliefs.
2. Josiah Coale, a Quaker preacher, offered to go with William to meet with his father.

3. When William took off his sword and gave it away, he was giving up the right to fight back and was following the Quaker tradition of nonviolence.

## Chapter Eight

1. *Barrage* means to direct an overwhelming outpouring, such as words or artillery fire, at someone or something.
2. The king decided to release William after he had written *Innocency with Her Open Face,* clarifying and explaining the beliefs that had offended church leadership in his earlier tract *The Sandy Foundation Shaken.*
3. The fact that a bishop could have William arrested for his religious beliefs shows that there was no separation between church and state.

## Chapter Nine

1. An indictment is a formal legal accusation.
2. The only charge the jury found William guilty of was speaking on Gracechurch Street.
3. The lord mayor ordered that the hats be put on so that he could accuse the Quakers of not removing them in the courtroom.

## Chapter Ten

1. *Prevailed* means overcame or triumphed.
2. John Bunyan is the author of *Pilgrim's Progress.*
3. The lord chief justice meant that a judge can try to influence a jury with arguments but he cannot use intimidation or threats to force them to reach a certain verdict against their conscience.

## Chapter Eleven

1. A proprietor is an owner.
2. The land was estimated to be 45,000 square miles.
3. William meant that he would not use his authority to take away any person's rights.

## Chapter Twelve

1. *Confiscated* means to have taken something away.
2. William named the new city Philadelphia, which means brotherly love. The name is a combination of two Greek words—*philos* (love) and *adelphos* (brother).
3. William paid for the property to show the Indians that he respected their rights and that he would be a fair governor.

## Chapter Thirteen

1. An edict is a decree or order.
2. William and Mary became king and queen.
3. William went into hiding because he was accused of treason and plotting to overthrow the monarchy.

## Chapter Fourteen

1. A tenant is someone who rents property.
2. Benjamin Fletcher, the governor of New York, was ordered to take over Pennsylvania.
3. The title of this essay was appropriate because William wrote it while in hiding.

## Chapter Fifteen

1. *Skeptical* means doubtful or uncertain.
2. William and the governors discussed the idea of a union of American colonies.

3. William meant that he wanted to run his colony without the interference of the English government.

## Chapter Sixteen

1. *Embodied* means fully represented or incorporated.
2. King William died after falling from his horse.
3. William collected goods produced by Pennsylvania colonists and sold them in London.

## Chapter Seventeen

1. *Lethargic* means sluggish.
2. William retreated to Ruscombe.
3. All royal charters were dissolved after the Revolutionary War because the colonies had become a united, independent nation rather than English territories.

# *Also from Janet and Geoff Benge...*

More adventure-filled biographies for ages 10 to 100!

*Abraham Lincoln: A New Birth of Freedom* • 1-883002-79-6
*Adoniram Judson: Bound for Burma* • 1-57658-161-6
*Amy Carmichael: Rescuer of Precious Gems* • 1-57658-018-0
*Betty Greene: Wings to Serve* • 1-57658-152-7
*Cameron Townsend: Good News in Every Language* • 1-57658-164-0
*Clara Barton: Courage under Fire* • 1-883002-50-8
*Corrie ten Boom: Keeper of the Angels' Den* • 1-57658-136-5
*Daniel Boone: Frontiersman* • 1-932096-09-4
*David Livingstone: Africa's Trailblazer* • 1-57658-153-5
*Eric Liddell: Something Greater Than Gold* • 1-57658-137-3
*George Müller: The Guardian of Bristol's Orphans* • 1-57658-145-4
*George Washington: True Patriot* • 1-883002-81-8
*George Washington Carver: From Slave to Scientist* • 1-883002-78-8
*Gladys Aylward: The Adventure of a Lifetime* • 1-57658-019-9
*Harriet Tubman: Freedombound* • 1-883002-90-7
*Hudson Taylor: Deep in the Heart of China* • 1-57658-016-4
*Ida Scudder: Healing Bodies, Touching Hearts* • 1-57658-285-X
*Jim Elliot: One Great Purpose* • 1-57658-146-2
*John Adams: Independence Forever* • 1-883002-51-6
*John Williams: Messenger of Peace* • 1-57658-256-6
*Jonathan Goforth: An Open Door in China* • 1-57658-174-8
*Hudson Taylor: Deep in the Heart of China* • 1-57658-016-4
*Lillian Trasher: The Greatest Wonder in Egypt* • 1-57658-305-8
*Lottie Moon: Giving Her All for China* • 1-57658-188-8
*Mary Slessor: Forward into Calabar* • 1-57658-148-9
*Meriwether Lewis: Off the Edge of the Map* • 1-883002-80-X
*Nate Saint: On a Wing and a Prayer* • 1-57658-017-2
*Rowland Bingham: Into Africa's Interior* • 1-57658-282-5
*Theodore Roosevelt: An American Original* • 1-932096-10-8
*Wilfred Grenfell: Fisher of Men* • 1-57658-292-2
*William Booth: Soup, Soap, and Salvation* • 1-57658-258-2
*William Carey: Obliged to Go* • 1-57658-147-0
*William Penn: Liberty and Justice for All* • 1-883002-82-6

*Unit Study Curriculum Guides are available for select biographies.*

Available from YWAM Publishing
1-800-922-2143 / www.ywampublishing.com